Euphemia McNaught/Pioneer Artist of the Peace

Isabel Perry

Euphemia McNaught
Pioneer Artist of the Peace

Isabel Perry

with the Beaverlodge & District Historical Association

Preface by Annora Brown

Introduction by Robert Guest, B.A., A.S.A.

A Reidmore Book

Horses Running Before Storm
17 1/2" x 26 1/2"   tempera on card   ca. 1935

Canadian Cataloguing in Publication Data

Perry, Isabel
    Euphemia McNaught, pioneer artist of the Peace

ISBN 0-919091-33-4

1. McNaught, Euphemia.
2. Painters - Canada - Biography.
I. McNaught, Euphemia.
II. Title.

ND249.M26P47   759.11   C83-091028-X

A Reidmore Book

Editorial   Marianne Lindvall-Morse
Design   R. G. Morse
Production   Van Campenhout Productions Ltd.
Typesetting   Horizon Line Typecraft Ltd.

Printed and bound in Canada

ACKNOWLEDGEMENTS

We are indebted to many people for aid in the preparation of this book, and to the officials of the Town of Beaverlodge, without whose support the project would never have begun.

Special thanks go to Dr. Robert Elliott, Betty Gaudin and Madelon Truax, who acted as the steering committee.

Our grateful appreciation to all picture owners, who so graciously loaned them for photographing.

Sincere thanks to Robert Guest, Doris Hunt, Evelyn McBryan, Mac McLean and Madelon Truax for contributing to the text, and to all those who helped with time, travelling and typing; Myrtle Guest, Pat Jacobs, Karen Martin, Doug and Doris McFarlane, Marilyn Snell, Gretta Schaffter and Al Truax.

DONORS

This book has been published, in part, through the
extraordinary generosity of
G. Douglas Mackie
and
Miss E. Jean Mackie

SPECIAL DONORS

Adrain, Jim & Louise
Alberta Advanced Education & Manpower
Alberta Art Foundation
Alberta Historical Resources Foundation
Anderson, Margaret E.
Andrews, Gerald S.
Archer, Mr. & Mrs. John
Astle, Gordon
Basaraba, Mr. & Mrs. George
Bask, Eric & Donna
Bateman, Mrs. Noriene
Bentum, A. V.
Bowes, Mr. & Mrs. William H.
Bristow, Mr. & Mrs. Edward
Bristow, Dr. & Mrs. Stanley
Burdon, Mrs. Olive
Burgess, Stephen F.
Burgess, Warwick
Burton, Mrs. Betty
Canadian Tire (Grande Prairie)
Carder, Dr. & Mrs. A. C.
Carter, Lock & Repka

City of Grande Prairie, Hugh Impey, Mayor
Collins, Mrs. Bea
Connelly, Caroline
Cottrell, Dr. D. G.
Dixon, Mrs. A. S.
Dixon, Mr. & Mrs. Donald
Elliott, Dr. & Mrs. C. R.
Emes, Mr. & Mrs. Leslie R.
Evashkevich, Paul & Coreen
Finistone, P.M.
Galusha, Sgt. J. Doug & Muriel
Garossino, Mr. & Mrs. R. C.
Gaudin, Mr. & Mrs. John I.
Gilliland, Alice
Grande Prairie Public Library
Guest, Mr. & Mrs. Robert
Gunderson, Mrs. Lillian
Hamel, Germaine M.
Harris, Rowe W.
Hartford, Mr. & Mrs. George
Henderson, Mr. & Mrs. G. M.
Hill, Mr. & Mrs. Vernon

Holroyd Drugs Ltd.
Hopkins, Viola
Howe, Mr. & Mrs. E. Wayne
Hughes, Mrs. Margaret
Humphrey, Mrs. C. E.
Hunkin, Dennis M.
Hunter, Rom & Lynda
Ireland, Mr. & Mrs. Guy
Irvine, Jean
Jacobs, Mr. & Mrs. C. P.
Jameson, Miss Eileen E.
Janzen, Herbert W.
Jewitt, Mr. & Mrs. Lloyd
Kirwin, Margaret and Biltek, David
Knox, Al
Koshman, Erroll & Catherine
Lee, Kelly
Lewis, Dr. M. T.
Loggie, Mr. W. P.
Lundblad, Lucy
MacDonell, Doreen L.
Madsen, Regeanne
Marshall, Gladys D.
Martin, Mrs. Karen
Martin, Mr. & Mrs. S. R.
McBain, Dorothy C.
McFarlane Agencies (67) Ltd.
McKay, Lillie V.
McMurray, Dr. Gordon L.
McNab, Don
Miller, Dr. & Mrs. David P.

Moore, Mrs. Sarah Anne
Morrison, Miss Florence
Moyer, Mrs. Edna P.
Murray, Arnold & June
Murray, Kim
Mutrie, Ms. Elaine
Nasedkin, Dr. John N.
Nielson, Anna R.
Nixon, Dr. James R.
Oatway, Dr. William A.
Ogren, Mr. & Mrs. A. H.
Oliver Funeral Chapel
Pharis, Lois Jean
Richens, Clifton W.
Rosenlund, Bruce and Terry Richens
Robinson, Cheryl
Rowles, Miss D.
Shank, Mrs. I. C.
Shea, Mr. & Mrs. James R.
Sherk, Don & Phyllis
Smith, B. Jean
Soltys, Amy
Spangelo, Mr. & Mrs. L. P. S.
Stacey, Mrs. Evelyn
Stacey, Mr. & Mrs. Hugh
Stretton, Mrs. D. Violet
Taylor, M. E.
Thompson, William
Truax, Mr. & Mrs. A.
Walker, Mrs. Margaret
Wanka, Maria Julia

Wilson, Mrs. G. M.
Wolfe, Dr. & Mrs. R.

Special donors who aided the association by participating in the art auction

Adrain, Jim
Adrian, Bill
Allingham, Harry
Beaverlodge Regional High School
Brown, Mrs. Marion
Collins, Mrs. Bea
Coutts, Marjorie
Dahlen, Laine
Davidson, John G. N.
Demuynck, Inez
Fellers, Mrs. Harriett
Gibson, Esther
Guest, Robert C.
Hamel, Germaine
Harpe, Alexander
Harris-Watt, Frances
Holroyd, Marion
Hotte, Mrs. Vicki
Hunter, Tom
Jewitt, Roger Law Office
Kohalyk, Anton
Lettington, Mrs. Jackie
Mackay, Phyllis

Marshall, Kathy
Martin, Karen
McBryan, Mrs. Evelyn
McIntyre, Fiena
McPhail, Edna
Millan, Reg
Moore, Ericka
Nordhagen, Mildred
Poole, Marvin
Radio Station CFGP
Radio Station CJXX
Randall, Marjorie
Reynolds, Doris
Schmidt, Mrs. Charlotte
Sheehan, Mrs. Beth
Shum, Wayne
Snell, Gary
Snell, Marilyn
Stewart, Colleen
Trider, Bernice
Truax, Madelon
Von Tiesenhausen, Peter
Von Tiesenhausen, Roman
Wagner, Mrs. Jean
Wanka, Maria J.

Thanks also to

Wallan's Auction Service
   (Glen Wallan, Franklin Hommy & Conrad Wrzosek)
Mr. & Mrs. George Carty
Dennis Tink

OWNERS

DEDICATION

Dedicated to the memory of Eliza and Charles McNaught,
our mother and father, to John, our brother,
and our two sisters Marion and Margaret.

PREFACE

To write a preface for a book of Euphemia (Betty) McNaught's work is a privilege and a pleasure. Our contacts of late have been sporadic, confined to letters, personally designed cards and occasional visits, but Betty's pervasive and consistent spirit has kept me in touch with the general trend of her work.

Arthur Lismer once wrote about the Group of Seven, "They took life seriously, art lightly and their Canadianism strenuously, but they were blithely unconscious of anything in the way of making history." These words apply with equal force to Betty McNaught, but there is a slight difference. When the members of the Group thought of Canada, they thought of northern Ontario and Quebec. To Betty Canada is her own region, far removed in distance and character from the East.

I first met Betty when we were students together at the Ontario College of Art in Toronto. There were five of us from the West, Betty McNaught (Peace River), Gwen Hutton (Calgary), Ruby Howe (Vernon), Dorothy Mason (Vancouver) and Annora Brown (southern Alberta). We loved Ontario and thrilled to the enthusiasm of such men as Arthur Lismer, A. Y. Jackson, J. E. H. MacDonald, Lawren Harris and J. W. Beatty. However, when they told us to paint Canada, our minds flew to our own areas — the real Canada.

Betty was the most vocal and dedicated among us. When we ought to have been absorbed with the task at hand, we were grouped around her listening to tales from her home.

She told us how her family had travelled by covered wagon over the Edson Trail, how her father had, at last, found an iron stake in the middle of nowhere and told them they were home, how the cattle had continued to move on each morning, accustomed to doing so, only to be rounded up in the evening. She told us how willow shrubs had been cleared to make room for a log cabin with a sod roof, that leaked forlornly with the melting snow in the springtime. They had had to stand on the bed, the only dry spot in the house, to get dressed in the morning! She told us how the cabin had eventually been replaced by a two-storey home with several outbuildings — all leak-proof. We got to know her animals by name and felt as if her family were our own. We learned about her neighbours, through her parents' concern for the welfare and growth of the community. In our imagination we attended the small school and the social functions, we rode with her sisters and friends to neighbouring villages, to the Red Willow and with packhorses to Monkman Pass.

At the College Betty majored in sculpture with Emmanuel Hahn as instructor. She produced beautiful heads and busts from living models, horses with intricate armatures and complicated castings in plaster. Her pen was busy too. We were all delighted by her drawings of the country she knew so well and of animals; horses on hilltops with manes blowing free, tired old packhorses, sturdy work teams.

The first year of the Depression was a discouraging time for a would-be artist to graduate. Betty taught

17

for a few years, then returned to Beaverlodge. Since the new community had no pressing need for monuments, Betty replaced clay and chisel with pen, brush and canvas. The knowledge gained from her three-dimensional work was evident in the solidity of form in all she portrayed.

An artist is more than an individual, who works with lines on paper and paint on canvas. Art is a way of life. To look at life with curiosity and wonder, to communicate experiences, makes life satisfying to the artist, and the artist of value to others.

To Betty home was a place where love of life was fostered and where joys and talents were shared with the community. One of the most significant sides of Betty is her love for all living things. She looks outward rather than inward. With clear, knowledgeable eyes she sees the trees, distances, animals and records them for all to love.

Arthur Lismer introduced Betty to the reed pen, which became a delicate extension of her fingers and her mind. Adapting his formula to her needs, she uses poplar cuttings for "reed" pens and combines the technique with underlying oil washes, which give rich lustre and a personal signature to her work. She is a realist in the best sense, showing her inner response to what her eye perceives with sensitive lines, shapes and rich colour.

The artist today is often separated from society. Not so Betty. In her art and approach to the community, she is dedicated to its service. Betty shares a home with her sister Isabel, an ardent potter specializing in native clays. They welcome groups of interested workers in their home. Betty has also helped to make an outstanding record of the early days in the Peace River Country through her historical, documentary paintings.

As a pioneer artist in a new country, Betty herself makes history. She has recorded for all times the spirit and forms of a vanished era.

For all this we thank you, Betty.

Annora Brown
Sidney, Vancouver Island, B.C.

18

INTRODUCTION

by Robert Guest, B.Ed., A.S.A.

Betty McNaught, a graduate of the Ontario College of Art, lives and works near Beaverlodge, Alberta, where she uses her environment as subject matter for her paintings.

Her art is very solid in connection with paint techniques, composition and the use of areas. She renders each aspect as a series of related areas. The paint is laid on directly, and texture is used to give each area its own personality. She creates the moods by using dark tones. One cannot help but sense the enjoyment she has in her environment and the pleasure, as well as interest, she derives from painting it in a very direct manner.

Betty was born at Glenmorris, Ontario, and moved with her family to homestead at Beaverlodge in 1912. They travelled to Edmonton and Edson by train, but the final journey north was by oxen and wagon over the Edson Trail. Her painting "Edson Trail Days" recalls the trip, made by many of the pioneers of the Peace.

Betty was painting already during her school years, convincing those around her that an artistic career would be a wise choice. Her family was aware of her talent, and Betty was encouraged to attend the best art college in Canada at that time. From 1925 to 1929 she studied at the Ontario College of Art in Toronto, graduating with the A.O.C.A. degree.

At the College she studied under a number of prominent Canadian artists, the best-known being J. E. H. MacDonald and Arthur Lismer of the Group of Seven.

At this particular time in Canadian history, a new artistic concept was in its developing stage. It went hand in hand with a new spirit of nationalism, following World War I. It was a search for Canadian identity. In essence the leading philosophy seems to have been, "to paint Canada not like the Europeans painted Europe." This attitude called for a bold, new look. Tom Thomson was likely the first Canadian painter who searched for, and achieved, a style that expressed the feeling of the rugged landscape. He used raw, brilliant colours, strong design and sculptural forms in a symbolic way, which soon caught on and led to a new Canadian style. The preference for the outdoors and for landscapes soon reached the student level at the art colleges. This is where Betty was exposed to a fresh, new way of painting Canada. However, she did not limit herself to landscapes.

In the early years of training, Betty's courses were general. She wanted to become an illustrator, but later specialized in modelling and painting. She was a four-time scholarship winner under the guidance of Emmanuel Hahn, who instructed sculpture, and MacDonald, who taught design and lettering.

The tempera illustration "Edson Trail" and the cast of a modelled piece, "Oxen Pulling Stump," date from this time. "Tom and Jerry" relates to the latter, but is a more complete, three-dimensional design. Although Betty's style reminds us of the Group of Seven, her themes are western and call to memory her own experiences in the Peace River Country.

After graduating from the College, Betty returned to teaching. Although she always seemed to enjoy groups of students, she was looking forward to the day when she would return to her art work. After a spell at Mount Royal College in Calgary and the Ontario Ladies College at Whitby, Betty returned to family and friends in Beaverlodge to stay and work with her family on the farm.

Her chief interest was initially in sculpture, but she soon discovered that there were few requests for monuments in smaller centres like Beaverlodge, especially in the thirties. Her emphasis changed to painting. The sculpture style was carried over into her paintings and drawings. She starts each composition by defining its structure with solid underpainting in dark tones, upon which she proceeds to construct her subject, usually in boldly applied colours.

Because a great deal of time had to be given to household chores and the caring of livestock on the farm, Betty developed a sure hand for drawing and a rapid style in painting, which enabled her to produce work quickly. This spontaneous quality is still a feature of her art.

Although trying to avoid long-term teaching commitments, Betty has conducted numerous workshops and classes in the area, many in her own home. She helped organize the Beaverlodge Art Club and is an active member in the Peace Watercolour Society.

Many drawings and sketches for future reference were done during the forties and fifties, when Betty saw a lot of the Peace River region travelling to such places as Hudson's Hope by mailtruck and into the Monkman Pass by packhorse. She gathered information in the form of well-composed drawings. Some were pencil, and others were drawn in ink with coloured pencil or watercolour wash.

At home Betty would quite often enlarge sketches to become oil paintings. "Allison's Mill," a choice theme taken from a spot along the Wapiti, "Old Fort St. John" and "Indian Graves" are examples of this. With a keen interest in local history, Betty became dedicated to recording landmarks that were fast disappearing.

She became a chronicler of the Peace River Country and the pioneer era. She has always been interested in the settlement, the new towns, the natives, the Monkman Pass project, and was an early traveller on the lower Alaska Highway, recording history in the making.

The Monkman Pass was to become a new route through the Rockies, connecting Rio Grande, Alberta, with Prince George, British Columbia. With the outbreak of World War II the ambitious project was forced to terminate. Betty was at the Monkman Pass making sketches, some of which were later painted. "Building A Bridge Over The Kinuseo" and "Trail Ride, Monkman Pass" are factual right down to the names of people and some of the horses!

Some sketches were done on location, such as the watercolour "Entrance To The Monkman Pass", in spite of the mosquitos! Some time later an important oil painting was inspired by the same theme. Its final version is one of Betty's most celebrated pieces.

Noticeable in this oil painting is Betty's love of design, lively colours, feeling for grandeur and space, all rendered in a variety of deliberate brush strokes that bind the picture together like a tapestry. Betty gives the landscape a glowing, sculptural quality, frequently seen in her studies of animals, buildings and people.

When the Alaska Highway was being built in the early forties, Betty was there recording the construction and military preparations. It was important to her to sketch the changes taking place because of war efforts along the Pacific Coast. But the sketches were more than records, they were works of art. Most of them combined pen drawing and coloured pencil or tempera wash. Her designs are clear and done with good contrast.

Considerable effort was required to gather this material; the roads were poor, the spots inaccesible, there were swarms of mosquitos and tight security around the military camps. Betty and Evelyn McBryan of Grande Prairie had obtained special passes to visit camps and army posts. Some works of both artists were later acquired by the Alberta Art Foundation.

Among Betty's accomplishments are "Maintenance Camp, Charlie Lake," a tempera painting including northern landscape and "Fort St. John," an ink and tempera sketch.

Betty's many sketches, including some finished works in coloured pencil, are usually rich and airy. "Azouzetta Lake" is done on a darkish green-grey paper. The rich colour and effective design are reminiscent of the Group of Seven. The mood is delightful here, where the ripples on the water surface and the contrast between far hills and mountains suggest the freshness following a rain. I have yet to see coloured drawing of this calibre anywhere.

From the mid-forties into the sixties Betty produced drawings in different media, including watercolours, Christmas card prints and oil paintings. Nearly all reflect her immediate surroundings and include horses, other farm animals, historic sites, farm homes, pets, people at work or resting and Peace

Country landscapes. Most of them show the McNaught sense of order, ease of touch and fascination with a local idea.

"Appaloosa" is a majestic study of a horse with her colt. "Edson Trail Days" was purchased by the Alberta Government for the Alberta Golden Jubilee Anthology in 1955. One of the most important paintings is "Indians Crossing Over Nose Mountain" from around 1950. It depicts a family of Beaver Indians returning to camping grounds on the Porcupine River from Rio Grande, where their baby had been christened at the Catholic Church. To reach their destination, they crossed over Nose Mountain, the grandmother carrying the child. Betty had seen the family on a trip with packhorses into the area long before there were roads into the vast, wild country south of Beaverlodge. This stunning composition is a landmark in Peace Country art. It is rich in colour, with boldly textured oil paint. It links Betty to the Group of Seven, but the theme is very western. Along with other work from Betty's production, this monumental painting could easily challenge the best work of her teachers.

"Dragga of Dumfrees" is a drawing, a tonal portrait of a dog, which also ranks very high. It is a reed pen drawing on brown paper, done with both black and white ink. This study represents a fine series of animal portraits, some of which were painted as well. The delicate "Stoney Lake" is an example of Betty's fine watercolours.

From the mid-sixties on, Betty has taken part in a wide range of projects, including illustrations for a set of local history books, "Beaverlodge To The Rockies" and its supplement. She has been able to complete many significant works despite her involvement in numerous community activities and art displays.

"McNaught Lake" marks a kind of departure for Betty. Previously she had applied oil paint as an impasto, partly for its textural effects. When "McNaught Lake" was done in the early seventies, she began to apply oil washes to her canvas boards. A drawing would then be carefully rendered in the popular reed pen manner, taking advantage of the canvas for subtle texture. The end result was a softly coloured pen drawing, which seemed to shimmer with a gentle, misty light.

Betty originally learned the reed pen technique from Arthur Lismer, but later substituted the reed with a poplar bough. Gradually her touch evolved and became a different form of drawing. She became a master of tone. Using nothing but a textured paper and black ink, Betty gives her compositions the feeling of depth and subtle detail, of which "Trees Where the Trail Divides" from 1975 is a good example. Her reed pen rendition is perhaps Betty's most original contribution to art in western Canada.

Betty frequently draws in pencil, partly to become familiar with a new theme. Some of her study drawings are masterful. "Smokey," the study of her own pony, done in fine line shading, is one example. In "George Brook's Cabin" a variety of pencils and strokes have been combined for a common effect.

Since Betty became a member of the Peace Watercolour Society in 1976, she has contributed to all its shows. "Old Trees On McNaught Lake" is representative of her watercolours, with a strong sense of design and a bolder colour scheme than earlier works. There is a kind of pre-winter melancholy in this delightful theme taken from the shores of the lake near Betty's home.

In all of Betty's work, there is a sense of place and a sense of new adventure. She believes in a broad style for a big country. Her colours are cheerful and express the excitement she feels about the Canadian landscape. Her animals, people, historic sites and portraits reflect a keen sense of design and a love for things that are genuine and close to earth.

Betty has truly pioneered art in the Peace River Country, and been recognized for her contribution to the visual arts with the 1977 Achievement Award and the 1982 Sir Frederick Haultain Award. She is also an inspiring teacher and one of the most optimistic people I have ever known.

*Isabel Perry
(née McNaught)*

It was around 1834 our great-grandfather John McNaught brought his family to Canada. He came to the Glenmorris area of Ontario, where there was a Scottish settlement along the Grand River called Dumfries.

Four sons and one daughter were with their father. Young John was an artist. He and his sister Margaret stayed on the farm. William moved to Atlanta and Samuel, our grandfather, got married and farmed near Brantford, Ontario.

Our father grew up there with his two brothers and one sister.

During the American Civil War William sent his family from Atlanta to stay at Glenmorris until the war was over. The cousins played together, rode the horses and formed friendships that were to last into the next generation.

Our father Charles married Eliza Conner, who lived near Brantford. The Conners were also pioneers, descendents of United Empire Loyalists. They bought a farm between Glenmorris and Ayr, and raised their family there.

John, Marion, Margaret, Betty and I spent our early years at this beautiful place. A creek made its way between the house and the barn. We were surrounded by woods and flowers, had all kinds of farm animals and a lake nearby.

Betty was not as fond of dolls as her sisters were, and did not play very much with them. When Mother read us books in the evenings, she would give Betty pencil and paper to keep her busy while she listened.

One night someone glanced at her drawing, laughed and passed it on. It was a drawing of a naked child with her long hair pinned into a knot on top of her head. There were little tendrils of hair escaping from the knot and even little curved lines for the ankle

bones. When we asked her about it, she said, "She's having her baff".

She might even equal the talent of her great-uncle John, whose painting hung in the parlour.

Sickness struck our family early on. After a session of carpenters remodelling our house, Betty came down with scarlet fever, followed by small pox. Mother looked after her and was finally so exhausted from the strain that the doctor prescribed for her a complete change of environment. Father suggested the Peace River Country in northern Alberta, and the doctor agreed it might be worth a try. Our uncle Sam had gone to the Peace earlier, with a group from Ontario, and spoke highly of it.

After University our brother John had taken a position with a school in Saskatchewan. He was now called home and left in charge of home and family together with his sister Marion.

Mother and Father boarded a train due west in June, bought oxen and buckboard in Edson and drove to Beaverlodge the first year the Edson Trail was open.

Mother's health improved and the Peace Country looked appealing. They filed on a homestead, bought a South African script of three hundred and twenty acres and arrived home in November.

When the final moving arrangements were made, and we had bid our sad farewells, the family left Ontario. Margaret and I stayed behind to continue our schooling.

The Chambers travelled with them, and together the two families had enough stock and goods to fill a freight car. The men rode with the belongings, while women and children took the passenger train. The party reached Edson by the time the snow was melting. The remaining journey over the Trail would have to wait until later in the spring. There were others with similar plans renting accommodation in Edson, while waiting for the grass to grow.

Finally the party was on the road, a rough, muddy track through the bush. The year was 1912.

They reached the stopping place on the Athabasca River in a few days. An ox took sick and died two weeks later, apparently as a result of a horse's kick. A party of three Irishmen came along with an ox, which had a broken toe. It could walk but not pull a load. Combining forces, they used the two good oxen, took one wagon and half a load each. The remaining goods were cached at the stopping place until they could return for them.

There were now three outfits in the party, the Irishmen, the Chambers and the McNaughts. Father drove the oxen, with Marion taking over while he was chopping a trail around the mudholes. It was slow going, as they had to double-up on the hills and over bad spots, while rough-locking down the steep hills.

The women and children found walking easier than riding in the wagons. The loads were heavy enough without them, and the children could make themselves useful driving the cows.

The chickens got used to the routine of being loose at night and loaded up for the day's travel. Oxen managed the mucky trail better than horses, because their cloven hooves did not act like suction cups as did the horses'. At night the oxen would eat grass, then lie down and chew their cuds and rest. The horses needed to eat longer, and missed their oats. Tents were raised at night, and when there wasn't time to set up the camp stove, cooking was done over a fire. Water and firewood were always readily available. In many ways it was a strenuous trip for man and beast; mudholes, corduroy, heat, mosquitos and camp cooking.

On a hot day everybody scrambled to get an early start and make use of the cool of the morning. During the mid-day heat, they made a long stop for dinner and rested in the shade. That evening they would travel into the night and make a late evening camp. When it rained, they stayed in camp, and precious time was lost. For the children, it was all an adventure; fun, excitement and absolutely no worries. Where the ferries had to make several trips across the river to transport a large party, the children enjoyed riding along on each crossing.

But travelling was slow, and the days were slipping by. Father and Mother had to report at the Land Office in Grande Prairie by July 1 or their land claims would be cancelled. From Sturgeon Lake they walked ahead to Grande Prairie and made it on time. When the rest of the party arrived with the wagons, Father had another ox ready. Two days later they forded the Beaverlodge River and drove on a few miles. Finally Father stopped. He looked around for the iron stake, got down to examine it more closely and said, "Well, if I can read this right, I guess we're home."

They made camp near the lake until they could choose a suitable building site.

A couple of young homesteaders stopped by as soon as they heard there was a new "skirt" in the valley. The nearest neighbour, Mrs. Mortwedt, brought a lovely fresh lettuce salad in a glass bowl. Aunt Lizzie McNaught came with a driving team to invite Marion to the three-day sports event at Lake Saskatoon. Marion was eager to go, and left to get ready. That was when she discovered that the wrong trunk had been left behind at the Athabasca stopping place. They had only their winter clothes along!

Our brother John was teaching in Manitoba by now. When school was out, a neighbour from Ontario joined him for the trip to Beaverlodge. They bought three horses at a ranch in Edmonton and arrived in Beaverlodge a couple of weeks after the rest of the family. There they sold the packhorse, but kept the other two, Lexie and Ginger.

Now there were horses to ride! Ginger was a sorrel, quite fast but given to bucking. Lexie was a chestnut-roan cayuse with the lines and grace of her Arab ancestors.

John and his neighbour Roy Maus stayed only a few weeks. They walked back to Edson, sending their packs on the mail wagon.

The first summer in Beaverlodge was a busy one. Father dug a shallow well and made a trip back to Edson for freight. He bought a set of logs and hired a man to build the house. He finished it just enough to allow the family to move in. A neighbour helped them with a small stable.

A new school district was being organized at Halcourt, and Marion was asked to teach for a few months until they could find a qualified teacher. Lexie and Ginger were ridden four miles to school and back every day. In a letter to us in Ontario, from our new home in the West, Betty made a drawing of Marion being bucked off by Ginger!

The following summer Father made yet another trip to Edson. He was to meet his sister Jane,

Margaret and myself. Margaret had spent the school year at the Calgary Normal School, and accepted the position as the first teacher in the Appleton School when it opened in the fall of 1913. Betty was her pupil. Since there was no high school in the area, I spent the following two years at home.

Betty and I had a great time. We rode the horses to the river for water, tethered them out to feed and rode on any errand available. A community basketball club was soon formed, and we rode to the practices with the odd horse race on the side. We went for raspberries, cranberries and blueberries.

One Halloween there was a dance at the Lower Beaverlodge School. A bunch of people gathered at our place and left their saddlehorses in our stable. As soon as they were off to the dance, Father and I took the lantern and went out to hunt for our cow Abigail, who had not come home with the others. We found her in the marsh at the edge of the lake. She had broken through the ice in an attempt to get a drink. Father tried to break the ice for her, but she was too cold to crawl out. We summoned a neighbour and got our oxen. Abigail had been so relieved to see us that she had started to chew her cud and aunt Jane put grass under her chin.

The oxen turned out to be of no use, since they simply got stuck in the mud. We needed manpower, so Father went west for the Foys, Dixons and Rays, while Betty and I rode north for Bert Elcombe. Eight or nine men finally managed to pull Abigail to shore. She was able to walk home, where we put her in the warmest stall with a blanket on. When the partygoers returned, Mary Ray found that her "horse" had grown horns and sported a blanket!

The following winter Father went out over the Trail for another year's supplies. Mother went along to look after him, since he had frozen his feet. She also intended to go to Edmonton for new glasses. We

Sunday he brought it to our place for Betty. When the others left for a picnic, we were warned not to ride the horse. We sat on the corral fence admiring the beautiful pony, who looked so friendly, and Betty could not resist. Robin soon became a member of the family and Betty's pride and joy. She would have been saved a lot of worry, had Mr. Robertson said right then that the pony was hers to keep.

four sisters were left alone to look after the place.

We were invited to a dance at the Rays one night. Since our only means of transportation were the two horses, we rode double. There was a guest at the party named Diamond Dick, as glamorous as his name and with a beautiful pinto only he could ride. He offered to ride home with Margaret when the dance was over. He ended up escorting both Margaret and Marion, each encumbered with a younger sister!

We had a surveyor visiting Margaret occasionally. Once he arranged to have a saddlehorse sent to him. It turned out to be too small for him to ride, so one

SMOKEY
ca. 12″ x 9″   pencil on paper   1976
SMOKEY
19 1/2″ x 14 1/4″   watercolour   1979

Betty continued drawing all through her childhood. Margaret, who had studied picture composition and the techniques of drawing in watercolour at Summer School, gave Betty her first real lessons.

Horses were Betty's favourite subject from the beginning, occasionally alternating with a special cat or dog. She once painted our oxen with show-card paint on cardboard. Any paper she could find had to do. However, the painting of the four of us riding to basketball was done on proper paper with good watercolours.

Basketball was very popular and many districts had their own teams. The practices were social events. Two teams of girls would play with rules and a coach, if possible, for half an hour. Then there would be a real game with mixed players, elastic rules and a referee to toss up the ball.

We Appleton girls were once scheduled to play at the Lake Saskatoon Sports. We decided to ride the sixteen miles there in the morning and play in the afternoon. However, that day the horses were not to be found until noon. We were late, but managed to hire a taxi from Beaverlodge. Fortunately we won and earned enough to pay the taxi bill.

Frank Donald owned a hotel and movie theatre in Grande Prairie. He once offered the whole team theatre tickets and supper if we would come play the Grande Prairie team. Thirty people made the trip and enjoyed his hospitality.

John was now the principal of the school in Pilot Mound, Manitoba. He sent for Mother and me to come there and let me take another year of high school. The following year he enlisted in the 196th Battalion and Mother, Betty and I moved to Calgary, where I attended the Calgary Normal School.

One day I approached my art instructor and got the name of an artist, who would take a look at some of Betty's work. Mr. Faux was very encouraging and Betty took a few lessons from him. Already we knew that Betty's future would be in art.

Betty attended high school in Lake Saskatoon. Four school districts had consolidated in order to run a two-room school, with grades up to and including XI, in an old flour mill by the lake. They were fortunate to have excellent teachers in the friendly village. In order to enjoy as much daily ice time as possible during the winter, the students were allowed to wear skates from the first recess on. A class thus encumbered with skates was surprisingly quiet! When John taught the high school, I arrived to take care of the Junior Room and expressed my surprise at the footwear. "Don't worry," said John, "It's a tradition".

Like the rest of us, Betty had her turn at the Calgary Normal School. When she came back, she was appointed to teach at Appleton. She stayed for two years, boarded at home and was back in the mainstream of community life again.

RIDING TO BASKETBALL PRACTICE
9" x 12" watercolour 1915

31

Tennis had now become quite popular. John and I had played a lot at Lake Saskatoon. Eventually courts were set up in Beaverlodge and Halcourt, where there were some keen players. Father built us a tennis court at home and our neighbours would join us there.

For several years Mother was instrumental in putting on garden parties at our home. The Women's Association and the I.O.D.E. women would organize the program and Father prepared the grounds to include a basketball court, tennis, clock golf and room for tables under the trees. The parties continued into evenings with a program of local talent.

When Betty had taught at Appleton for two years, she had saved up enough money for a year at the Ontario College of Art in Toronto.

Doris Hunt

The whole family was aware of Betty's ability, and it was an established tradition that sons and daughters of the Valley went "outside" for training beyond high school. John encouraged Betty to attend the best art school available at that time in Canada.

Isabel Perry

I decided to take a year off teaching and go along. I would stay only if I could find a job. When we arrived in Toronto, we went first to the Y.W.C.A., bought a newspaper and a map. We quickly found a housekeeping room in the vicinity of the University and the Art College. I got myself a job at an art novelty studio, where they produced hand-painted lampshades.

As soon as we were settled, we called our friends, Dr. and Jean Carlisle. We asked Jean about coming events in the entertainment field and for best buys in suitable clothing. She suggested good coats and hats first of all. We immediately took our new fox and coyote furs from the North to a tailor to have them made up with the then-so-popular soft velour.

Her first day at the College, Betty looked around at

a long hall full of strange faces. In front of her in line stood a tall, beautiful girl. Their paths happened to cross often those first few days and a lasting friendship developed. Marie Guard came from Port Credit and was also alone. Soon Gwen Hutton from Calgary, Ruby Howe from Vernon and Annora Brown from McLeod joined the group.

The girls took their homework and the recommended side trips seriously. They went to the museum, the zoo, on outdoor sketching excursions, to exhibitions, and I joined the group for some of this. We also added a few outings for fun. We went to Sunnyside Amusement Park to have a ride on everything we could afford. We went to the Hunt Club Carnival and the Royal Winter Fair. We saw Lon Chaney in "Phantom of the Opera," live ballet, "Blossom Time" and "Rose Marie."

A HARD WINTER
9 1/2" x 13 1/4" watercolour on paper 1920

The Art Gallery had an exhibition of the Group of Seven's paintings, and Betty and I were there. It was a wonderful experience. Betty was so fortunate to have several of these artists as instructors and Tom Thomson's work as an inspiration.

Betty and her college friends often went on weekend sketching trips. Carrying lunches and sketch-boxes, they would board a streetcar and ride it as far as it would go.

We had some wonderful afternoons at Port Credit with Marie, her parents and sister Margaret. Annora's aunt, Mrs. Bowerman, often brightened our Sunday afternoons with teas in front of the fireplace in her beautiful livingroom.

Groups formed around shared interests at the College. Betty found herself surrounded by seven girls, four of whom came from Alberta. These four, and roommate Anne Warwick, remained close associates throughout the years in Toronto.

They were the Westerners, who marvelled at the rich fall colours and the densely packed scenery in the East.

One weekend Betty and I went to Bronte to visit our cousin Grace Mackie, her husband Leonard and children Jean and Douglas. They were very interested in the Peace River Country and later bought land beside ours south of Beaverlodge. Many years later, when Betty was honoured with the Alberta Achievement Award in 1977, Jean entertained her with a dinner in Calgary.

At the end of Betty's first College year, awards were given out at the Toronto Art Gallery. The hard-working Westerners all received scholarships along with their certificate scrolls. Betty's was in Lettering and Design, which she had studied under the famous J. E. H. MacDonald.

We had made up our minds to spend our carefully saved ticket money on a car and drive home. No mean feat in 1925. We bought ourselves a second-hand 1919 Model T and left it in storage until Easter time. Then we took it for a trial run to Brantford to visit relatives. I had wanted a lesson in city driving, but the man from the garage only came with us past Younge Street, where he left us by the City Hall. We knew that a car was not supposed to pass a stopped streetcar, so, to avoid mistakes, we stayed behind one for miles until we were out of the city.

We named the car Prudence.

When the College year ended in late May, Annora Brown agreed to come with us in the car. We joined the A.M.A. and planned to follow the Yellowstone Highway.

We picked our camping equipment frugally and packed it carefully. Marie Guard and her sister came with us to the Niagara Falls, where we spent the day. They took a boat back to Toronto and we crossed the border into the U.S.A.

We had a flat tire at Lake Erie and had to buy a new one at a garage. We had stopped in front of a fire station, where several men were at hand to help us change tires. The car did not have removable rims, so we had to pry the tire off, remove the innertube, put it back on and pump it up with about three hundred strokes. We eventually became quite proficient.

In Wisconsin we had our first encounter with

Madelon Truax

Isabel Perry

the June bugs. With the car's headlights directed at our camp, Annora was in trouble, with ninety percent of the area's insects settling in her bright blonde hair!

The trip was unforgettable. We saw the country more thoroughly, and met more interesting people, than one would on a modern-day car trip.

In Glacier National Park we had to have our car repaired. It was our first time in the mountains, and we thoroughly enjoyed the drive north. We entered Alberta at Babb and left Annora at her home in McLeod. In Calgary we stopped to visit our cousin and his wife, Major and Mrs. Stuart. Since we had run into cold, rainy weather, we not only enjoyed their warm welcome, but also their warm house!

From Calgary we headed east through Drumheller to Delia, where our sister Marion and her husband George Martin lived. What a happy reunion we had with them, their

daughters Peggy and Janet and our other sister Margaret, who was teaching in Delia. We went to a dance in the country and had a picnic — just like home!

Our last stop was Edmonton. The road north from there was very poor, and we decided to sell our car and take the train.

By this time Betty was determined to return to the College for three more years. The family would give financial assistance, if Betty could help with the seeding and harvesting. As it turned out, she won scholarships in modelling each of the three following years, so tuition was not as heavy an expense as had been anticipated.

But life at home was not all work. Since cars were still not plentiful, we formed a riding club and rode to picnics and on exploring trips together. We carried lunches and made tea over the campfire. Quite often we found our way to Perry's river land and enjoyed its winding cattle trails and scenic camping spots. Sometimes we would go out for an entire weekend.

In the fall Betty returned to Toronto for her second year. Marie Guard had gone to New York for a course, but the others were back. Betty boarded at the Y.W.C.A., where her room-mate was Anne Warwick from Blenham, Ontario. Dorothy Mason, a third-year student from Victoria, and Annora Brown also stayed at the "Y". They formed a close little circle.

With some coaxing, the treasurer Maude Fleming arranged that they would all eat with her at one table. That's the way it remained for Betty's years in Toronto.

The old Elm Street "Y" was a very special place. Miss Ross, the secretary, ran it like a college residence. Sunday evenings there were music, prayers and always an interesting speaker. The girls themselves took part in plays and musical entertainment. One memorable event was the annual Ghost Walk through the huge, dungeon-like basement, a theme we used years later for a moonlight hike on an island in our lake at home.

The girls at the "Y" also enjoyed their eating parties after lights were out at eleven o'clock p.m. Mother used to send food parcels as special treats. Little did she know that they were sometimes finished under the beds in Betty and Anne's room! On one such occasion, an explosion rang out into the night from the big front window, sending the girls scurrying into the hall with "blood" on their feet. The much-dreaded Miss Myers came immediately, investigated the room — and discovered the ketchup! Mother had sent a special kind that the girls had cached too close to the steam radiator, causing the bottle to explode.

Betty's Toronto years formed many happy memories. One involves the annual tea dance for the college students in the studio of Mr. Reid's home. Others derive from times when Arthur Lismer and J. E. H. Mac-Donald selected students to be entertained by Lawren Harris in his studio. Sitting around on the floor entranced by his charm and sincere philosophy, these students began to see that the composition and glowing light of his later paintings were the results of the depth of his thoughts. They felt fortunate to be in Toronto at this time. Herbert Stanfield taught a course in basic design, followed by advanced uses of design in enamelling and jewelry making. J. M. Beatty had such a thorough understanding of composition, colour and texture in his own work that it was an inspiration to try to follow him.

These instructors impressed their students with the need for thinking in terms of the "elements of art," space, form, texture and colour. Using the basic

shapes of a line, circle, square or triangle or the form of a sphere, cube, slab, cone or pyramid, the artist starts his creation.

Betty's work reflects this approach; it is rich in shapes, colour and texture. Each tree is a specific shape, each branch a shape within a shape, created by colour and texture. When Betty paints a tree, she draws the skeleton in heavily with dark paint. Then, shade by shade, with thick paint rolling from her brush, she creates texture and highlights the way only a master of the technique can.

Isabel Perry

Arthur Lismer was one lecturer in a thousand, who, with keen wit and colourful words, could make a History of Art class entertaining. While correcting someone's poor foreground, he once said, "The trouble with you Westerners is that you can't see close up for gazing into the distance." Another time he commented, "It takes two people to paint a picture; one to do the painting and one to knock him on the head when it is finished."

Madelon Truax

Isabel Perry

Madelon Truax

In Betty's fourth year at the College, Lismer gave a short, extra-curricular course in the use of the reed pen to some of the students.

He used pens cut from reeds that grew around Toronto. When the course was finished, he gave each student a supply of pens to start out with. Years later Betty was on a pack trip to Monkman Pass, when she lost her last reed pen. Alex Watt, a member of the party, said, "Oh, any old poplar will do!" and proceeded to cut Betty a pen from a tree branch. Poplar twigs have since been Betty's favourite "reed" pens.

Madelon Truax

She sharpens the end of the twig slantingly, dips it in India ink, draws her picture in long strokes and shades it with halftones obtained as the ink gradually dries on her pen.

Over the years the reed pen has become one of Betty's favourite tools, and the resultant creations some of her most valued work. Over a period of time she has added her own dimension to what she originally learned from Lismer.

She uses the reed pen on a background of oil wash or light spraying of delicate shades of lavender, rose, blue and green. This emplasizes a decorative style, which increases the depth of the central form. The coloured backgrounds add a misty, transluscent aurora to her pictures.

The Art College Graduation Night program was held in the Toronto Art Gallery. Betty's friends were all among the eight honour graduates, who received the degree Associate of the Ontario College of Art (A.O.C.A.). Betty's scroll read, "General Proficiency With Special Mention For Modelling." She hoped that Emmanuel Hahn had added the mention of her modelling.

Mr. Hahn was a prominent figure on the small eastern Canadian sculpture scene and, in Betty's opinion, the best sculptor in the country. He instilled in his students the importance of solid form and structure with the same vigour the Group of Seven gave to landscape painting.

For all Betty's work with watercolours, tempera, oils, reed pen and crayon resists, her first love remains sculpture and reliefs done in clay.

From Betty's second year at the College, she found herself drawn more and more to this medium, encouraged by her scholarships and by Hahn, who was known to be quite critical of his students. He wanted them to be able to create work so decisive that thumb textures would be imprinted in their pieces.

Two beautiful reliefs hang over Betty's fireplace; "Lars Haukeness and His Horses" and "Tom and Jerry." The latter shows a team of oxen straining in

LARS HAUKENESS
25" x 34"   plaster cast   1935

their harness. They had been very special oxen to the family, having been brought in over the Edson Trail.

The strong, skillful modelling of the curve of neck and head, the muscles of shoulders and haunches, express the power of these draught animals and the determination of man and beast necessary to carry the homesteaders through the month-long journey over scarcely-broken trails.

Betty's style reveals a sculptor's mind in a number of ways. Her preoccupation with form implies a subordination of the colour sense to the sense of structure.

It makes Betty prefer tempera over watercolour and encourages the use of the reed pen. Both mediums lend themselves to Betty's "building-up" technique. "Build up the composition," "build-up the form" and "get depth into it" are expressions that describe her artistic processes.

Betty's modelling skill has also given her pictorial style its most marked characteristics. Her habit of thinking in terms of form and structure makes for a distinctly sculptural quality in her painting.

Graduation Day in 1929 brought mixed feelings. Betty and her associates were proud of their success, but knew this day meant the parting of their ways. Annora, Gwen, Ruby, Anne, Ken Drummond, Mac McLean and some others suggested a reunion every ten years. As it turned out, only Annora, Gwen and Ruby kept in touch, the rest contributing the odd card.

Ken Drummond once drove west with a reunion in mind. He and Betty drove to Vernon only to find that Ruby (Howe) Henry had died several years earlier.

They did not find Gwen (Hutton) Lamont in Kelowna. But, near Sidney on Vancouver Island, Annora Brown welcomed them at her beautiful cottage. Dorothy Mason joined them there.

Mac McLean and his wife also drove west, gathering information for the College Alumni.

Betty has on separate occasions visited Annora, Gwen, Mac, Ken and Anne (Warwick) Blair.

Still, on that graduation night, there was a creeping feeling of emptiness. Each graduate returned home after four memorable years. Betty came back to Beaverlodge and once again became deeply involved in the life of her community.

Her art is closely linked to the Peace River Country, a varied landscape composed of a series of natural prairies separated from one another, and the outside, by vast forests. The Grande Prairie, in which Beaverlodge is situated, is the largest one. It is an expanse of rolling plains broken by a profusion of fruit-bearing shrubs, by bluffs of spruce intermingled with poplar and balm-of-gilead, by small prairie lakes and by the many winding tributaries of the Smoky and the Peace. The skyline toward the west is formed by the jagged blue crest of the Rocky Mountains.

"Indians Crossing Over Nose Mountain" is a crisp, cool rendition of a group of Beaver Indians crossing the crest of the mountain on their way from Rio Grande to camping grounds on the Porcupine River. The bodies of the horses form a composition of graceful curves against the broad expanse of wind-swept sky.

In "Horses Running Before a Storm" the presence of more animals is suggested by limiting the canvas to

Doris Hunt

Doris Hunt

Isabel Perry

three or four horses against a dramatic backdrop. The rhythm of limbs and manes, the curve of the hilltop and the sweep of clouds above express the pulsating excitement of the herd racing before an approaching storm.

Domestic animals play an important role, but do not monopolize Betty's attention. In a locale where wildlife abounds, it is not surprising that one of her strongest animal paintings is "Moose on the Wapiti." Occupying almost the entire canvas, in bold relief against a sunset background and the rugged banks of the river, stands the majestic figure of a bull moose.

The Peace River Country also provides source material for Betty's historical collection, which, apart from its artistic merit, has considerable documentary value. The landmarks she preserves on canvas are fast disappearing.

Isabel Perry

Betty McNaught
for Art College paper

Many pioneers of the Peace look back with regret, most finding that they were too busy to keep any record of the early years. The scenes from then remain only as mental pictures, brought to life again by the fireside. They again see hot days and long lines of wagons, drawn by panting horses and oxen knee-deep in mud or rattling over rough corduroy. They see them paused for rest on a hilltop after a long climb. They see the slow, ponderous ferries crossing the rivers with their loads — the cattle too tired to be afraid, and the children too excited to be tired.

In camp at night a huge fire's flickering light blurs the faces. Some are listening to a story well told, others joining in the songs or just enjoying the quietness and a chance to rest after a long day. Faintly they can hear the clear cow bells, the swish of the dark river below and trees above.

They relive the winter scenes; the long, narrow trail ahead, making its way through moss-draped spruce onto a bright clearing with a low log stopping house and stables set deeply in the snow banks. They can feel the clear, sharp mornings, with sleigh runners groaning and oxen white-coated with frost.

These may seem like only memories, but they can be beautifully told on canvas. The old trails, the sunken stopping houses, the deserted homesteads telling stories of high hopes that did not last until the coming of the railroad. There lies a country, fresh from the dawn, pulsating with life and colour, just awaiting the painter's brush.

Betty's references from the Ontario College of Art soon resulted in a position as an art teacher at Calgary's Mount Royal College. She stayed there for two years, and enjoyed it immensely.

She was used to the residence routine after her years in Toronto, but still wished the kitchen staff a good night her first day on the premises!

The art teacher was not required to preside over the study hall, but was instead given charge of the Friday night social with the girls. Betty enjoyed this and the basketball games, occasionally featuring the Edmonton Grads.

A badminton court was situated across the street. The students were allowed to book times there, or accompany friends on visiting lists. Betty was in charge of the girls, a male colleague the boys. To avoid having the girls slip out on her, Betty decided to run a tournament every badminton night. The students would choose their own partners, and the remainder were paired off as appropriately as possible. This may not have been college policy, but the administration did not mind. At least they had no runaways!

Margaret Carrick, Dean of Girls, dietician and part-time painter, loved the foothill country west of Calgary. The College's secretary, Mr. Walters, and engineering teacher, Major Richards, often arranged sketching trips to scenic, out-of-the-way places. One Saturday a party drove to Bragg Creek with lunches and sketch boxes. Local Indians had just tied their horses to some trees outside a small store. Betty's tempera painting "Bragg Creek Horses" was painted that day.

Doris Hunt from Winnipeg and Alice Hockins from near Halifax joined Betty on many foothill excursions. They also spent time in the studio. Doris was just back from a scholarship year in Paris and wanted to continue her training. At one time she came to Beaverlodge to spend a month with Betty. They spent the time sketching, including a week at Hudson's Hope. They caught a ride in with mailman Les Baisley, and came out again a week later via Fort St. John. Doris, who is a very organized person, had decided on "seven days for seven sketches." Betty's seventh is still unfinished — but she tried.

They had rented an attractive log cabin and at the end of the week invited their newly-found friends for coffee, a good-bye and an exhibition.

In the early thirties Betty received a telephone call from a Grande Prairie girl named Evelyn Newton McBryan. She had recently been married, and her husband was encouraging her to pursue her artistic talent. A small news item in a local paper, about Euphemia McNaught returning from Mount Royal College, gave Evelyn the incentive to call. Since Miss McNaught had been the College's art teacher, she would perhaps take on a student.

This phone call marked the beginning of a long friendship, and was the initial move toward the formation of Grande Prairie's first Art Club.

It was arranged that Evelyn would take the Tuesday train to Beaverlodge and wait at the grocery store until Betty's brother John could pick her up. She would stay at the farm Tuesday and Wednesday nights, returning to Grande Prairie on Thursday's train. This became a monthly ritual for years.

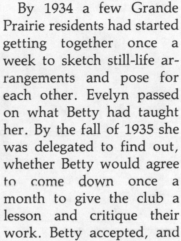

The trip from Beaverlodge to the McNaught farm gave John and Evelyn ample opportunity to "solve the world's problems," discuss the new talkies at the movies (Eddie Cantor in "Making Whoopee" took up one trip alone!) and any other subject under the sun. A trip by horses and cutter, with Peter and Poky pulling, supplied enough time. In the summertime the trip was made in a Model A Ford.

Betty's lessons were serious and enlightening, fitted around a busy schedule of feeding livestock and helping with the cooking.

By 1934 a few Grande Prairie residents had started getting together once a week to sketch still-life arrangements and pose for each other. Evelyn passed on what Betty had taught her. By the fall of 1935 she was delegated to find out, whether Betty would agree to come down once a month to give the club a lesson and critique their work. Betty accepted, and the Grande Prairie Art Club was off and running.

Membership fluctuated, but a solid core of people remained constant. These decided they needed more help. Betty responded by arranging Grande Prairie's first Art Workshop.

Frank Donald donated the use of an empty building he owned on Richmond Avenue. The participants brought their own wood and coal to keep from freezing, and Mr. Donald even sent one of his men with firewood. The Workshop included drawing, painting, composition, colour theory, batik, clay modelling and plaster casting as well as lino block printing. It started at 9:00 a.m.; the participants brought lunch and supper and stayed until midnight.

What prompted the long hours is hard to say. It could have been industry and a thirst for knowledge, or simply the survival instinct; it was necessary to

Evelyn McBryan

keep the fire going twenty-four hours a day to keep frostbite at bay. By banking the stove up with coal at night and sending Evelyn's husband Harry over at 7:30 a.m. to start the fires, they managed. Water was carried by the bucket from the hotel across the street.

Arthur Lismer had been to Edmonton on a lecture tour. Betty's sister Marion had talked with him, and brought word home that the Ontario Ladies College at Whitby was looking for an art teacher. Betty applied for the job, was accepted and spent two happy years at Whitby. The beautiful Elizabethan-style College building was part of a hundred-acre farm with extensive grounds, barns, a garden, pasture and orchard. The produce from the farm helped the College through the thirties.

There was room for six riding horses, and teachers with previous equestrian experience were allowed to ride after school hours. Betty and her friends would travel along back lanes, on either side of the Kingston Highway and down by the shore of Lake Ontario. On one such ride they stopped for tea with the art teacher at the Mental Hospital. The horses were tied to the guard fence in the parking lot behind the residence. When the guests returned, they found some older patients running their hands gently over the satin smooth necks and velvet noses of the quiet

horses. Betty felt sorry for these men, so obviously missing a country life they had once enjoyed. She wished there could be farms available, where people could experience — if only for a weekend — a walk on soft paths in the woods, the sound of horses, cows and sheep eating their night-time hay.

The Ontario Ladies College at Whitby was a wonderful place. Miss Maxwell and Dr. Carscallen carried on the traditional routines alongside modern courses of study. Disciplinary measures were superfluous, since no one ever stepped out of line.

Each class chose their own "class teacher," and the graduating class asked Betty to be theirs at the beginning of her second year. She told them she was pleased, but was also a bit uncertain as to what precisely this honour would entail. The class president assured her, "Don't worry. We would like to have you, and we will tell you what to do."

Marion Rickard from Bowmanville had a room across the hall from Betty. She was fresh out of the Toronto University, so was also treading lightly. She gave Betty one word of advice; never enter a room without pausing to size up the situation at hand.

The warning came in handy at the end of the second year. Betty and the graduating class president

WHITBY LADIES COLLEGE
24" x 28"   tempera & coloured pencil on card   ca. 1935

had the task of leading the way down the aisle to the graduating service in the United Church. There were three aisles. Betty remembered in time to hesitate and allow the president to step forward into the right line.

When Betty returned home at the end of her second year at Whitby, she found that Father had a serious heart condition. We all spent as much time as possible at home that summer. Marion and her two girls stayed the entire summer, with George joining them for his three-week vacation. Margaret was teaching not too far away. The two men helping on the farm kept Father informed of the happenings of the day. It was a warm summer, and we often had tea under the trees beside the house. Neighbours dropped by to share this time with us. Whitby at that point felt very far away, so Betty wrote to Dr. Carscallen and sent in her resignation.

One afternoon Father woke up from a deep sleep and said to Marion, who was sitting there sewing, "I have just come back from a long way. I think this is the way it will be."

Later that fall Father slipped quietly away.

Betty stayed at home to paint after Father's death. I married Jud Perry the next year. When our daughter Liza was two years old, Jud died and I went back to teaching at a local school. Liza stayed at home with the family on the farm. She became an ardent, self-taught skier, and rode her quiet horse Sharon on the cattle paths along the lake.

Breakfast was a good time at the farm; a time for talking and for planning the day. Betty would get up early to serve the men breakfast, then sit down later with Mother and Liza. In the evenings Betty and

Mother would read aloud. Friday evenings were special to us all, since that was when Margaret and I returned home for the weekend.

A few years later Mother died.

The years at home gave Betty free time for sketching trips, since the farmwork was shared by many. John and our cousin Crosbie McNaught owned three quarter-sections of river land along the Red Willow, where they pastured horses and cattle. Near that river we built a cabin, which we still enjoy. Liza and her cousin Marjorie Hunkin spent much of their holiday time riding there, checking on the cattle and looking after the horses. This gave Betty a chance to escape the confusion of a busy farm. She would accompany the girls to the cabin, and while they rode she painted.

Although times had changed and cars had become plentiful, our horses remained important to us. We loved to ride. One summer Marion, Olga Kolosoff from the Beaverlodge Reasearch Station and I went with our neighbours, the Dixons, on a pack trip to the mountains. We had found our brother John's old packsaddle, and he had shown us how to tie a diamond hitch to hold the pack. We accompanied the Dixon party to the top of Nose Mountain some ninety miles away and came back by ourselves.

This was the first of many trips into the mountains. We were usually seven or eight to a party, using four packhorses. John came along on one early trip, and Betty on the next.

One memorable trip brought us via the Monkman Pass to the Kinuseo Falls on the Murray River. We brought a map and filled in the details with the help of a trapper, who lived along the route. It was a rugged — but beautiful — trip. The last half had not been travelled much, and we had to cut our way through the occasional tree across the path. But we were well rewarded for our struggles. The view of the Kinuseo Falls, fifty feet higher than the Niagara, with the mountains rising beyond, was wonderful.

I made good use of my camera. The photos were used the following year, when the Monkman Pass Association was formed to promote the building of a railway through the pass.

Doris Hunt

The Peace River Country, initially the frontier of the fur trade and Indian missions, quickly gained a reputation as an important grain-growing area, despite the transportation costs involved. If a railway were to be put through the Monkman Pass, Vancouver would not be much farther off than Edmonton. The Association expressed the need for an outlet to the sea in an organized fashion and started a unique road-building project.

To demonstrate that the Monkman Pass was highly feasible, it undertook to build a road to the top of the Pass using only local labour and equipment. Betty recorded what might well have been an epoch-making period in the life of the region. This portion of her work includes a panoramic view of the Pass, a reed pen study of trees along the Murray River and an oil of a construction gang laying a log bridge across a mountain stream.

Isabel Perry

On the trip to see the volunteer work parties, we took no packhorses, since three of us rode in the wagon with the supplies. We made our last camp at the Kinuseo River, close to the bridge building site. Some of our party stayed there, while five of us walked on some twenty miles to Monkman Lake. This was only a few miles from the summit of the Pass. It looked like rain, and we were forced to turn back in case the Murray River rose. The drops began to fall, and we took shelter under a spruce tree,

the men dashing out in the dark now and then for wood to keep the fire going. Betty and I walked back to sketch and photograph in the morning. At lunch time we caught up with the party and got safely back to camp.

By this time the Monkman Pass Association had proven the practicality of the route, but had run out of money. The British Columbia government was not prepared to cooperate and the war had started, requiring both men and money. When the war was over, there was a railway under construction through the Pine Pass, effectively scuttling the Monkman route.

In 1939 Peggy Martin, Virginia McDonald, Stan Haliday, Jim Harcourt, Bruce Albright and Betty took a packhorse and walked from the Kinuseo Falls to Monkman Lake. They carried meagre provisions, intending to live for two days on fish, huckleberries and Sunnyboy cereal. While the rest of the party fished and picked berries, Betty collected material for her painting "Monkman Lake."

In Toronto we had seen the Hunt Club Carnival and the Royal Winter Fair, which inspired us to put on a musical ride at home. There were enough people in the area to have sixteen riders. Since we did have some experience training children for drills in Christmas school concerts, we had the riders practice on foot before we used the horses.

We put on the show in our pasture, with the Beaverlodge Band supplying the music. It went over well, and we put on another show the next year, adding to it Musical Chairs with audience participation and the Air Force Band from Grande Prairie. The third year, our Ride was invited to participate in the Beaverlodge Sports with twenty-four riders and the help of Madelon and Al Truax, the Edgertons, Jonas Webber and Margaret Harris.

We also copied the Ghost Walk, which Betty remembered from the Y.W.C.A. in Toronto. One moonlit autumn night we invited guests to a party at our lake. A ghost guided them, in small groups, across a mossy strip to a spruce-clad island. There another ghost took them through haunted, clanking trees to a lighter area, where a bear — almost — attacked them! The bear was Harold McSherry in Al Truax's fur coat. The ghosts vanished later on, and the guests were left to find their way back alone. Madelon ended up using the same place and arrangements for a party for her neighbourhood a few days later.

World War II had both terminated the Monkman Pass project and instigated the building of the Alaska Highway. The entire Peace River region was swept up in the excitement surrounding this huge project, and Betty, of course, hastened to record the developments with her brush.

She and Evelyn McBryan had discussed the possibility of recording this epic construction project, but neither knew how to go about obtaining permits to enter the military construction camps. One night the local MP, Mr. Jack Sissons, was visiting the McBryans and saw some of Evelyn's sketches. He suggested, too, that the building of the highway ought to be in some way recorded. He told Evelyn how to proceed regarding permits, and offered to vouch for the artists.

The arrangements resulted in three trips by car during the summers of the early forties, and one trip in 1947, when permits were no longer necessary.

Betty's sketches from this period include one of the Peace River bridge, of the maintenance camp at Charlie Lake and Fort Alcan, the sup-

ply base for the highway. They are more than simply records. Each one is a piece of art. Most of them combine pen drawing and coloured pencil or tempera wash, with clear designs and excellent contrast. This, combined with the nostalgic interest of the works, recording as they do scenes that no longer exist, made their purchase by the Alberta Art Foundation a natural acquisition. They were later placed on permanent loan to Grande Prairie's Prairie Gallery, together with Evelyn McBryan's work from the same period.

Betty and Evelyn continued to paint together, but with less frequency as the years progressed. When Evelyn McBryan became the arts and crafts coordinator for the City of Grande Prairie, she was instrumental in arranging Betty's first solo exhibition at the Arts and Crafts Centre in 1970, the start of a wider recognition of Betty McNaught's work.

After Betty had moved home to paint full-time, she needed a place to work. The house was always full. It so happened that the Appleton school, where she had both attended and taught, was for sale. Betty bought it for fifteen dollars, and had it moved to our farm. The hand-hewn logs, enormous beams and south wall of windows made a fine studio, as well as a community centre.

On one special occasion people gathered there to meet A. Y. Jackson and Francis Loring on their return trip from the Alaska Highway. They had given a talk at the Beaverlodge Community Centre and followed

Evelyn McBryan

Evelyn McBryan

Isabel Perry

Doris Hunt

up with coffee at our place later.

Only while spending three years in charge of the School for Retarded Children in Grande Prairie did Betty set aside her painting and work with art clubs temporarily.

Madelon Truax

Betty's Christmas card printing project has developed into a unique part of her artwork. Some years she cuts stencils and uses spray paint to transfer her designs to cards. Other years she puts her design on heavy linoleum, chips away the background to make the subject matter stand out, inks it over and presses it on cards that have been sprayed with a blend of paints. When the blocking is done, a few brush strokes highlight certain areas. Her cards are framed, hung and treasured by many friends.

Isabel Perry

In the early sixties the University of Alberta, reacting to a growing interest in art in the Peace Country, arranged a University Week in Beaverlodge. This was to become an annual event. The lecture programs were varied, including discussions on politics and world problems. People came from miles around to hear speakers such as Colonel Cormack and Dr. Johns. Betty was also among the lecturers. She was asked to give a talk and a demonstration of her work. The following year she expanded her presentation to include other local people, who, through their talent and interest in the arts, photography and crafts, had made contributions to the community. Due to interest shown, and the availability of a Community Centre in Beaverlodge, the Department of Extension decided to run a six-week program of courses in pottery, woodwork and weaving. This was a great success and resulted in the formation of the Beaverlodge Craft Club, still in existence. The same Department was responsible for the visual arts travelling collection's annual tours around the province. Betty's work was included.

In the mid-sixties Les Graf and the Department of

Extension also arranged for Betty to hold courses at Peace River, High Prairie, Spirit River, Fairview and Grande Prairie. The stops were far apart, but Betty managed by giving lessons at each centre once a month. She would give a talk and a demonstration, then assign extensive homework. Those who brought in complete material received a critique; those who did not, came to listen.

Evelyn McBryan at one point agreed to make a feasibility study concerning the interest for an arts society in the Peace region. She reported her findings to a representative group at Fairview, and as a result the Peace Region Arts Society was organized. It included five zones of the region, each represented by three culturally involved individuals on the council.

The organization flourished for years, but the travelling distance between the zones hampered the work. The council was eventually put on the shelf, but out of its efforts grew the Peace River Arts Festival. All five districts, with the addition of Dawson Creek in British Columbia, join together for the festival to take part in music, drama, writing, arts and crafts. Whenever possible the districts take turns hosting it, but all zones exhibit work. Fairview College has hosted it twice, Beaverlodge twice.

One day Betty received a telephone call from Madelon Truax of Beaverlodge. Her sister-in-law had sent her a sketch box and the advice, "If you want to have fun in your spare time — paint!" Madelon was enthused and turned to Betty for advice on how to get started. From this small beginning the still-flourishing Beaverlodge Art Club was born.

Betty began giving classes in her home to a small group of people, some of whom have continued to come once a week over the years. The class structure eventually turned into a club, where a core of interested and talented individuals got together to paint and talk. At seven o'clock every Tuesday evening the session begins in the studio, to conclude several hours later with a snack and Irish Coffee.

When weather so permits, the club members sketch

outdoors, at old building sites or other local scenes. All the members show their work at local exhibits and find an increasing demand for it.

Provincial awards bestowed on Betty serve to underscore the far-reaching value of her contributions, both as a producing regional artist and an exceptional instructor. The Peace Country arts scene would look very differently indeed without her enthusiastic presence. She has instructed workshops and art classes for years, is a member of the Peace Watercolour Society, continues to guide and critique her club members and enjoys an increasing prominence on the western national arts scenes.

Betty, drawing from her own training at the Ontario College of Art, always stresses to her students the use of shapes and forms, asking them to relate all objects to their simplest level; circle, cone, square, triangle. The arrangement of these forms and the spaces behind them must be complimentary and realistic.

No one can say about a McNaught painting, "The perspective isn't right." Whether Betty is composing her own work or helping a student, her primary question is, "Where is your eye level?" Once it is established, a few swift lines will outline the perspective as a guide to keeping the picture realistic. To find the correct place for her centre of interest, Betty draws a diagonal line from one corner to the opposite one of a rectangle. From a third corner she drops a line perpendicular to the diagonal line. Where the two lines intersect, lies the centre of interest; not in the middle of the picture, not halfway up or down, but at the pleasing spot found by her method.

Betty advocates a "pyramidal" composition. This means an arrangement where one point in the picture is higher than the rest; all main forms and shapes must stay below that point.

Colour is also important to Betty. She is not afraid to use strong, vibrant colours but remembers always their relationship to each other on the colour chart, greying them when necessary with opposites. She never uses black for this purpose, insisting that it deadens the tone.

She pays tremendous attention to texture. She loads her brush with paint and lays it on in strong, definite strokes, letting the roll of the brush create ridges of texture, which, under her subtle control, add depth and drama to the painting.

By changing colours and laying one beside the other, she forces the eye to blend them — not the brush! This, quite simply, is the touch of a master.

Betty has created her own unique approach to oil painting by creating richness with texture and vibrant colours.

Her major source of material since her childhood and student days has been animals. Her second interest is local history. In her lifetime she has seen the changes wrought in an isolated community by the coming of a railway, the building of schools, the development of medical services and the opening of a highway to the far north. She is perhaps more conscious of social change than an artist living in a more complex society, thus her work chronicling old buildings, homesteads and the

Madelon Truax

Doris Hunt

Monkman Pass and Alaska Highway projects. While Betty is clearly an artist firmly rooted in the past and present of the Peace River Country, her art is not mere visual journalism, but art that both focuses on and transcends the regional.

Madelon Truax

Tumbler Ridge is, in this vein, a new area that Betty is exploring and preserving with her painting. The town of Tumbler Ridge sits in the magnificently wild and rugged terrain of the foothills, overlooking the confluence of the Murray River and Flatbed Creek. Discoveries of massive coal deposits in the Rockies have opened up new vistas for trade and commerce, as well as for the artist. The excitement and activity of yet another frontier lures the pioneering spirit within Betty McNaught.

Isabel Perry

As she finished her first Tumbler Ridge painting, complete with a surveyor stake in the foreground, she challenged the Beaverlodge Art Club to invade the area with her. Her enthusiasm never fails to inspire others to take on material from new areas.

This adventurous streak aside, Betty has always found a great deal of material on her very doorstep. Her artistic eye has turned many a humble scene into a composition of true splendor. She has never had to go far for excellent subjects, and besides, her most loyal buying public prefers the "local scene."

Betty still lives on the farm near Beaverlodge. From her kitchen window she can see the Rocky Mountains sparkle in the distance. Closer lie rolling hills and vast grain fields interspersed with parkland bluffs. In the immediate foreground her beloved horses scatter sheep and chickens, and cows rest beneath the huge spruce trees that seem to thrive on the edge of McNaught Lake. Trumpeter swans nest in the reeds, and beaver build their dams to keep the water level high. "No hunting" signs posted around the property allow Betty to catch glimpses of deer or moose browsing through the winter on the edge of the lake.

This lake, along which Father and Mother camped their first night in the Peace, is not a recreational lake. We treasure it more for the birds, its adjacent pasture, beautiful water and trees. Two spruce-and-poplar-covered islands, with willows and cat-tails, supply a good variety of material for Betty's outdoor sketching.

The beauty is now being disturbed by beavers, who have moved in and are cutting down and drowning trees. Muskrats have been residents for years, but live unassumingly and cause no harm. Hundreds of ducks, and one pair of swans, bring up their young on the lake every year.

A few years ago an old mother swan died, leaving the father to raise the young. He did, and flew south with

THE McNAUGHT HOME, BEAVERLODGE AREA
7 1/2" x 10 1/2"   oil on panel   ca. 1930

them when the time came. Three swans returned the next spring, but soon there were only two. The third one might very well have been the old one with nothing better to do than join a singles' club!

One year in the early sixties the swans on McNaught Lake were disturbed by the noise of nearby road construction. Our neighbour called up and said, "Come quick, girls! There are five baby swans walking along the highway, and the traffic is thick." Margaret and Liza drove straight to the spot, gathered up the little ones and brought them home.

From that moment on they were people to us — not swans.

We telephoned local naturalist Bernard Hamm to tell him what had happened. He concluded nature must have made a mistake; usually only one parent bird moults at a time to avoid leaving the eggs alone. Since we were dealing here with the near-extinct trumpeter swan, Hamm called Ottawa to report the case. There the response was disappointing; the swans would have to be put back in the lake.

Mr. Hamm knew, and we knew, that the swans would not survive on their own in the lake. Young swans get water-logged very quickly, and are then easy prey for coyotes. In Ottawa they knew nothing about this; they didn't know our lake. A man was sent up from Edmonton to make sure the orders from Ottawa were carried out. With her feet dragging, Betty helped

carry the swans out in his boat to be set down on the open water like little decoys.

The following morning our neighbour Ern Dixon called again: "Come right away! The swans are back on the highway." We drove around to the same spot, and the birds flopped toward us as fast as they could. Bernard Hamm called Ottawa again, this time with a different message. This was the year of the swan.

We dug out a swimming pond in our front lawn and lined it with heavy plastic. A small pen and partial shelter served the birds at night. Hundreds of people came to get a glimpse of the cygnets, to our knowledge the only ones in domestic care. Their growth and behavioural patterns were recorded on film by Frank Darby, the local station agent. The swans soon learned to come when called, waddle down to the pond, swim a while and return for their milk and bread in front of the visitors. Their faces were so individual that we knew them by name.

They would have made fine artist's models, but were a bit uncooperative. If one sat down, all five wanted to sit down in one feathery pile. If one stood up, they were soon all faces and legs.

Fall came, and tragedy struck. One swan was to be sent to Calgary and one to Saskatchewan. The three remaining were to be let loose at Lake Saskatoon, where the wild swans gather before going south. These three were released and may have survived. The other two died of lead poisoning.

They had been in the habit of walking with John through the garden, practicing flying as they went along. At the rubbish pile they would stop and pick up stuff to eat. There is a possibility they ingested lead, which had leaked from discarded car batteries. Margaret and John sat up with them the night they died. Margaret never could enjoy looking at the slides of the swans after that.

The Peace River Country probably looks much as it did years before people came to disturb it. The shapes of valleys, hills, rivers and mountains don't change. Only the surface has changed in pattern and texture. Prairies have become grain fields, bush land has been cleared for home sites and roads have created a squared-off pattern across it all.

Betty says, "I like perspective. I like the way the forms have been textured with this organized pattern."

At night the dark loneliness and wide-open spaces are warmed by the lights from small towns along the highways. The communities are growing, changing and extending. Distances have shortened and life has become easier.

People in the Peace are able to join in the national interest in, and consciousness of, art. The opportunity to travel outside to paint, make local artists aware and appreciative of their own surroundings. It enables them to paint their area, with greater sensitivity.

Improved communications have also made local artists recognized well beyond their own region. Betty showed the way.

Three of her paintings and four sketches were acquired by the Alberta Art Foundation for the Jubilee Collection, the beginning of the Government Art Collection. She has had two paintings exhibited at the National Art Gallery, and one in the 1955 Alberta Golden Jubilee Anthology. The province has recognized her contribution to the visual arts on two occasions, in 1977 with the Achievement Award and in 1982 by making her the first recipient in art of the Sir Frederick Haultain Award.

She is among the best-known of the many stout-hearted pioneers, who represent the Peace River Country. Not only did she come in over the Edson Trail as a child, but was later recognized in a different sense.

Euphemia McNaught has pioneered art in the Peace!

McNaught Lake, East Shore
20" x 26"   oil on canvas   1981

SALLY ON HORSE
15 1/2″ x 19 3/4″   watercolour   1977

A Boy and His Horse
19″ x 15″   oil on panel   1979

HORSES AND CUTTER
ca. 9″ x 12″   pencil on card   1977

52

HORSES AND CUTTER
5 1/4" x 7 1/4"   oil on panel   ca. 1945

53

54

CATS
16″ x 12″   crayon resist   1970

McDuff

16″ x 12″   crayon resist on paper   1976

EDSON TRAIL DAYS
20″ x 30″   tempera   1927

EDSON TRAIL DAYS
N/S   oil on canvas   ca. 1954

TREES, McNAUGHT LAKE
30″ x 23 3/4″   reed pen & oil wash   1964

OLD TREES ON McNAUGHT LAKE
13 1/2″ x 19 3/4″   watercolour   1979

Cabins Across the Wapiti
11 3/4″ x 15 1/4″   oil on panel   1981

JIM CAMERON'S CABIN, MOONLIGHT
18" x 24"   oil on panel   1979

ADAM KENNY'S CABIN
10" x 14"   oil on panel   1977

TRAPPER'S CABIN
13″ x 16″   reed pen   ca. 1950

TAYLOR FLATS
12″ x 18″   pen & coloured pencil   1947

HALCOURT ANGLICAN CHURCH, SKETCH
14" x 18"   oil on panel   1980

DUDLEY SHAW'S CABIN
13 1/2″ x 15″   pen & coloured pencil   1922

66

CARL BROOK'S CABIN
11" x 17" watercolour 1980

HUDSON HOPE, MAIN STREET
12″ x 18″   steel pen & coloured pencil   1949

THE HENDERSON PLACE
13 1/2″ x 19 3/4″   watercolour   1980

St. Mark's Church, Appleton
8 1/2" x 11"   oil on panel   1927

PEACE RIVER ANGLICAN CHURCH
13″ x 15″   ca. 1956

OLD FORT ST. JOHN
9″ x 13″   tempera on card   1945

72

ALLISON'S MILL
16″ x 20″   oil on panel   1965

WORK FARM AT CHARLIE LAKE
14″ x 20″   coloured pencil   1946

THE ART CHAPMAN PLACE
14″ x 21 1/4″   watercolour   1980

75

Moose
24″ x 30″   tempera   1939

MARGARET'S TURKEYS
15 3/4" x 19 1/2"   crayon resist   1981

DEER
30″ x 24″   pen & oil wash   1964

DEER ON SPRUCE ISLAND
15″ x 24″   watercolour   ca. 1975

79

OUR COWS
21″ x 28″   watercolour   1981

Horses on the Hill
16 3/4" x 21 3/4"   watercolour   1981

HORSES GOING TO WATER No. 2
4″ x 6″   watercolour   1950

Running Horses
10 1/2″ x 15 3/4″   oil on simulated canvas   1976

TANSEY
17 1/2″ x 14″   oil wash   1972

CHIEF
14″ x 20″   watercolour   1977

HORSES
31 1/2″ x 22″   oil on burlap   1964

86

APPALOOSA

20″ x 16″   oil on canvas board   ca. 1950

Lars Haukeness
25" x 34"   plaster cast   1935

Horses Going to Water
10 1/4" x 14 3/4"   ink & coloured pencil   1952

LITTLE DORRATT
13″ x 18″   oil on canvas   1960

Horses Across Valley to Nose Mountain
19 1/4" x 30"   oil on panel   1971

Nose Mountain
16″ x 20″   oil on canvas   ca. 1950

92

MONKMAN LAKE
24″ x 30″   oil wash on wood   1942

PACK HORSE
12″ x 9″   crayon on paper   1915

NIGHT CAMP, NOSE MOUNTAIN
24″ x 36″   oil on canvas   1981

SKETCH FOR ENTRANCE TO MONKMAN PASS
13 1/2″ x 17″   watercolour on paper   1939

ENTRANCE TO MONKMAN PASS
24″ x 30″   oil on wood   1950

FINLEY FORKS
16″ x 20″   oil   1971

98

Euphemia McNaught.

WAPITI RIVER
10″ x 14″   oil on panel   1979

Junction of Peace & Smoky Rivers
N/S   oil on panel   1950

SCHOOL MURAL
48″ x 96″   oil   1967

Old Red Willow Trail
15″ x 20″   watercolour   1976

BLUEBERRY PICKERS
11 3/4" x 15 1/2" reed pen & oil 1979

MUSKEG ALONG KINUSEO RIVER
24″ x 36″   oil on canvas   1970

McNaught Lake by Moonlight
24″ x 36″   oil on panel   1972

Poplars, McNaught Lake, Fall
13 1/2" x 19 1/2"   watercolour   1978

STONEY LAKE
13 1/2″ x 21″   oil on burlap   1971

STONEY LAKE
15″ x 20″   watercolour   1976

Trees, Wapiti River
20″ x 14″   reed pen, sprayed background   1980

Moberly Lake
12″ x 18″   oil on panel   1964

BEAVER DAM
12″ x 24″   oil on panel   1975

Two Lakes
20″ x 30″   oil on panel   1975

STURGEON LAKE
20″ x 36″   oil   1980

CREEK NEAR HONEYMOON BRIDGE
N/S   reed pen & coloured pencil   1965

114

BURL TREE, MOONLIGHT
28″ x 23″   reed pen & oil wash   1978

SPRUCE ISLAND
15″ x 30″   oil on panel   1980

116

BURL TREE IN MOONLIGHT
16″ x 20″   reed pen   1979

STONEY LAKE, MOONLIGHT
16 1/2″ x 30″ oil on burlap 1969

Beaver Dam on Monkman Pass
24″ x 36″   oil on panel   ca. 1970

119

BRAGG CREEK
13 3/4″ x 19 1/4″   tempera on card   1934

INDIAN GRAVES AT HUDSON HOPE
13" x 20"   watercolour   1981

121

Maple Trees
13″ ✕ 16 1/2″   oil on panel   ca. 1930

122

MIXED TREES
10 1/2″ x 13 1/2″   oil on panel   ca. 1930

AZOUZETTA LAKE
12″ x 18″   coloured pencil on tinted paper   ca. 1955

124

BEAVERLODGE VALLEY
14 1/2″ x 21 1/2″   ink & coloured pencil   1968

125

Fort Saint John
N/S   pen & tempera   ca. 1943

MAINTENANCE CAMP, CHARLIE LAKE
N/S   tempera on card   ca. 1943